# Flowers

by Giulia Verzariu
illustrated by Lorinda Cauley

Pre-Decodable 12



McGraw Hill Education

Bothell, WA • Chicago, IL • Columbus, OH • New York, NY

**MHEonline.com**



Send all inquiries to:
McGraw-Hill Education
8787 Orion Place
Columbus, OH 43240

ISBN: 978-0-02-145281-1
MHID: 0-02-145281-4

Printed in the United States of America.

7 8 9 LCR 25 24 23

You see  .

red flowers

You see 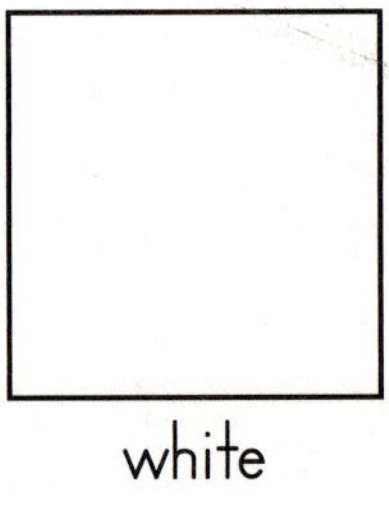 .

white flowers

You see  .

yellow flowers

You see  .

purple flowers

You see orange  flowers.

I see  !

flowers

I see you!